Dedicated to all the wonderful, kind, caring people that
have helped Henry and me throughout this journey.

Written by Hilary Seif
Designed by Dana Viglietta

Printed by CreateSpace, An Amazon.com Company
www.CreateSpace.com/5783648

Available from Amazon.com, CreateSpace.com, and other retail outlets

Henry

a very
SPECIAL PUP

WRITTEN BY HILARY SEIF
DESIGNED BY DANA VIGLIETTA

It was a beautiful spring day and I was in the puppy pen playing with all my brothers and sisters when I heard the door open and someone say, "Pick whichever puppy you want."

Then I heard another voice say, "I want that one! He's cute and looks special." I was then scooped up, and off I went to live in my new home.

MY name is Henry and I'm a GOLDenDOODLe.

Little did my mom know how "special" I'd turn out to be!

The first day in my new home was scary.

I kept running into everything, like furniture and walls.
My mom would laugh, pick me up and say,

"OH HENRY...
YOU'RE SUCH A CLUMSY PUPPY!"

As I got used to my new house, I discovered it was so nice. I had lots of fun toys and a really nice bedroom with a big comfortable bed and a soft blanket.

Soon after we got home, my mom said I had to go see a doctor. Mom says all puppies go get an exam when they go to their new home, just to make sure they're healthy.

Dog doctors are called veterinarians, or "vets" for short. I was scared to go to the vet, but my mom said she would be with me the entire time and I'd be all right.

When we got to the doctor's office, mom held me while the vet examined me. He looked in my ears and my mouth. He looked at my paws and gently squeezed me all over.

IT TICKLED A LITTLE WHICH MADE ME WAG MY TAIL!

Finally, the vet opened my eyes and shined a bright
light in them. Taking a deep breath, he said, "oh no!"

"WE HAVE A PROBLEM. HENRY HAS CATARACTS AND HE IS BLIND."

My vet explained that because my eyes were all
cloudy, I couldn't see anything.

Now it was my *mom* who was scared! She held me close and I licked her nose, giving her kisses to let her know that I was going to be fine.

The vet suggested we go see a special eye doctor for animals called a veterinary ophthalmologist. So the next day we went to see the new doctor.

I liked it as soon as I walked in! The people who worked there were super nice to me and I felt like a movie star when I strolled in, and everyone said,

"Here comes Henry Doodle!"

They gave me lots of love and even some doggie treats!

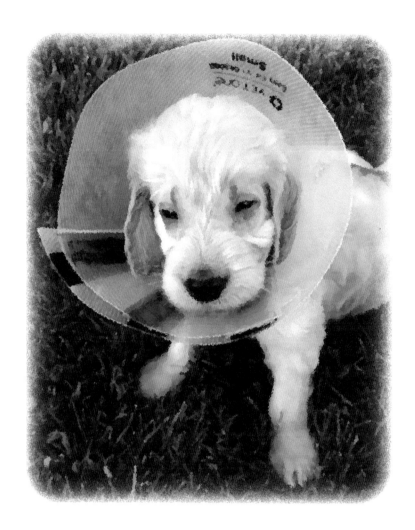

My new doctor looked in my eyes and said she could do surgery and put a new lens in each eye to help me see. So the very next morning, I had surgery. When I woke up from surgery I saw my doctor looking at me and smiling.

YEP! I COULD SEE HER!

I couldn't wait to see my mom and go home and look at all my toys. When I got home, I went into the back yard to play. I not only smelled the flowers and the grass – I actually SAW them for the very first time.

The grass was so green and the colorful flowers were beautiful.

I was one Happy Puppy!

Over the next few months, mom and I were quite busy. She said it was time for me to go to school and learn some manners and be trained to be on my best behavior.

I was one
PROUD PUP!

School was so much fun and my teachers were so cool! They taught me how to sit and stay and how to come when called.

At the end of my training I got a certificate saying I graduated puppy school. Everyone clapped for me, and my picture was taken with my teachers and my certificate.

When I wasn't at school, I stayed busy playing with my friends and the neighborhood kids.

I loved to play outside in the yard, chasing the ball and squirrels. If I wasn't busy all the time, I'd get bored and dig a hole in the yard just for fun. Mom was not amused.

Digging holes caused me to get in trouble and have to go to time out. Mom says it's not good to dig holes. I think it is fun to dig them and hide my bones.

My favorite game is called "keep-away." It's so much fun! I get something that doesn't belong to me and then I run around and around the trees or a couch, and whoever is playing the game with me chases me!

"KEEP-AWAY" IS THE BEST GAME EVER!

It was just a few months after my first surgery that I woke up one morning and didn't feel very good and my eyes hurt really bad.

Mom was worried so she called my eye doctor.

We went to see her that same day, and she said they had bad news for us. The doctor said I have an eye disease and would have to have surgery again to make me feel better.

MOM WAS SO SAD.

She cried the day of my surgery.

When I woke up this time, something was different.

I ONLY HAD ONE EYE.

They had to remove an eye in order to get rid of the horrible pain it was causing me.

Having one eye isn't so bad. I might have a disability, but it doesn't keep me from doing all the usual things I do.

I still play and run and jump and bark. I run into things sometimes – and it hurts – but I shake it off and go on with my day.

I LOVE SEEING
MY EYE DOCTOR!

My friends at the pet store showed me some really cool toys that make noises, so I can find them when I play in the yard.

I have a toy duck that goes, "Quack, quack, quack," until I find it in the yard or house. Mom tries to hide it so it's harder for me to locate, but I always find it and come running back with my duck in my mouth.

 SHe can't FOOL me!

Sometimes life isn't so much fun, like when people call me names, such as, "Pirate Dog," or "The One-Eyed Bandit." I just ignore them.

Grandma says if people don't have anything nice to say, they shouldn't say anything at all. I tend to agree with her.

Every month I get to go to the eye doctor and have my left eye checked for the same disease that took my right eye. The doctor has prepared my mom and me that the left eye will eventually have to be removed when the pain gets too bad.

But until that day, I'm going to run and play and chase squirrels and HAVE FUN!

I'm going to live life to its fullest!

MY name IS Henry and I'm
a SPECIAL GOLDENDOODLE!